Classic Cars *of* Old Havana, Cuba

A TRAVEL PHOTO ART BOOK

LAINE CUNNINGHAM

Classic Cars of Old Havana, Cuba

A Travel Photo Art Book

Published by Sun Dogs Creations
Changing the World One Book at a Time
Print ISBN: 978-1-951389-12-3

Cover Image by Laine Cunningham
Cover Design by Angel Leya

Copyright © 2024 Laine Cunningham

All rights reserved. No part of this book may be reproduced in any form or by any means, electronic, mechanical, digital, photocopying or recording, except for the inclusion in a review, without permission in writing from the publisher.

Old Havana, a UNESCO World Heritage site, has a lot to offer. One of the most unique and fun attractions moves through the city's streets. Old Havana's classic cars, many of which are convertibles, stand out with colorful pops of pink and red.

Drivers of perfectly restored vehicles can follow routes proposed by their riders. They might recommend certain routes based on interests like architecture or a cruise along the Malecon seawall. These pristine models navigate the same streets as lovingly restored ride-hailing cars and well-worn colectivos.

Grab a ride in these vintage models to taste the true flavor of Cuba.

BEAM

GANGSTER

GLORY

SURVIVOR

SWEET

THRUM

NIBBLE

PEERS

PERCHED

TOOLBOX

TAFFY

STOCKPILE

MENTHOL

CHEWY

BEACH

CHEVRON

EYES

DRAGONFLY

BOLD

PONTOON

PURSE

TUSK

RIDER

GRASSHOPPER

WAZZUP

DARTS

AERO

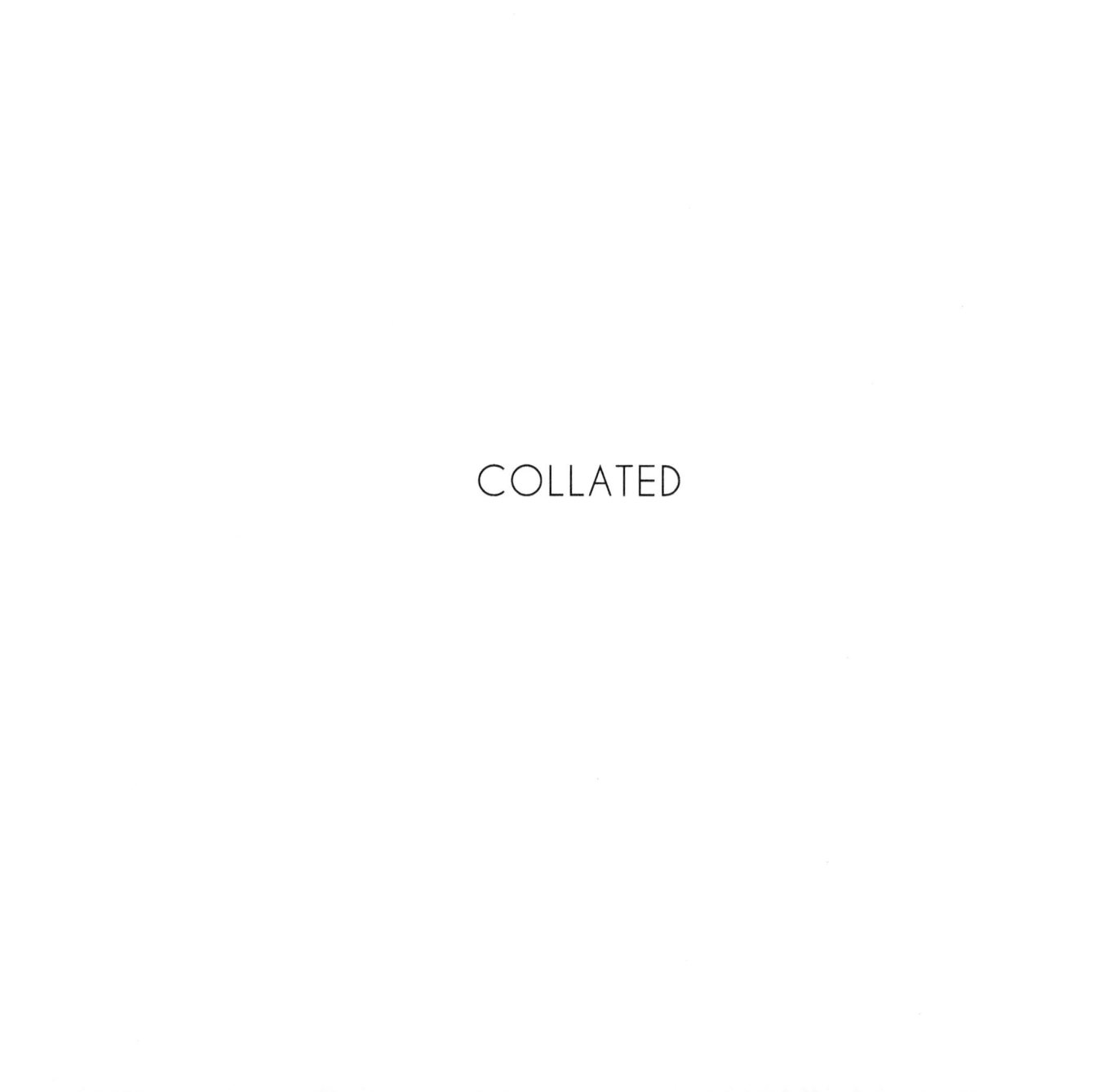

HAVANA

DECKED

PEEK

GOLDEN

FEDORA

BARREL

HONORABLE

LOPE

JUMPSTART

TRIUMPHANT

HISTORIC

BLOWFISH

MONOCHROME

ARBITER

CRISP

WINNER

TITLES IN THIS SERIES

Havana, Cuba
Old Havana, Cuba
The Malecon, Havana, Cuba
Central Havana, Cuba
Vedado, Havana, Cuba
Regla, Havana, Cuba
Miramar, Havana, Cuba
Streets of Havana, Cuba
Classic Cars of Cuba
Classic Cars of Old Havana, Cuba
Classic Cars of Havana, Cuba
Spanish Colonial Havana, Cuba
Gardens of Havana, Cuba
Verge Gardens of Havana, Cuba
Cats of Havana, Cuba

www.ingramcontent.com/pod-product-compliance
Lightning Source LLC
Chambersburg PA
CBHW040001080526
44586CB00027B/2846